DATE DUE

The Library Store   #47-0103 Pre-Gummed

Young
Arthur Ashe

Brave Champion

A Troll First-Start® Biography

by Robin Dexter
illustrated by R.W. Alley

Troll Associates

Library of Congress Cataloging-in-Publication Data

Dexter, Robin.
  Young Arthur Ashe: brave champion / by Robin Dexter; illustrated
by R.W. Alley.
      p.   cm.— (A Troll first-start biography)
  Summary: A brief biography of the African-American tennis champion
who died of AIDS in 1993.
    ISBN 0-8167-3772-X (lib. bdg.)   ISBN 0-8167-3773-8 (pbk.)
    1. Ashe, Arthur—Childhood and youth—Juvenile literature.
2. Tennis players—United States—Biography—Juvenile literature.
[1. Ashe, Arthur.   2. Tennis players.   3. Afro-Americans—
Biography.]   I. Alley, R.W. (Robert W.), ill.   II. Title.
III. Series.
GV994.A7D49   1996
92—dc20
[796.342'092]
[B]   95-10021

Printed in the United States of America.

10 9 8 7 6 5 4 3 2 1

Arthur Ashe was a champion tennis
player. He won many tournaments. He
also won the hearts of people all over the
world by helping others.

Arthur Ashe, Jr. was born in 1943, in Richmond, Virginia. His family had been in America since 1735, when one of his ancestors was brought from West Africa as a slave.

In 1863, during the Civil War, President Abraham Lincoln freed the slaves. But that did not end the troubles of African-Americans.

When Arthur was born, Southern
communities were segregated. White
people had separate schools from black
people. They even had separate playgrounds.

Arthur grew up in a house near a large
playground for blacks only. There were
four tennis courts there. That was where
Arthur learned to play.

Arthur had a younger brother, Johnnie.
Arthur's father was a park policeman. Mr.
Ashe had to raise his sons by himself.
Arthur's mother had died when Arthur
was only 6 years old.

Mr. Ashe took his sons to church every
Sunday. He made sure they learned to
help others. Sometimes Arthur went with
his father to bring clothes and food to
families in need.

Other boys in Arthur's neighborhood
played football. But Mr. Ashe would not let
Arthur play because he was not very big
or strong. Instead, he gave his son a
tennis racket.

Once Mr. Ashe saw Arthur get angry and
throw his tennis racket on the ground.
The next thing Arthur knew, his father
was marching over to the tennis court!
Arthur never threw another racket.

When Arthur was 10, Dr. Robert Walter
Johnson, Jr. began coaching him. Dr.
Johnson taught him how to play tennis
well. Arthur learned how to stay calm and
be polite on the court.

This self-control helped Dr. Johnson's players win. A player who gets angry can lose his concentration—and lose the game.

13

Arthur played against other black children in local park tournaments. But because of segregation, he was not allowed to play in city tournaments. Those were for white children only.

When Arthur was 17, he went to live in St. Louis, Missouri, where he could practice with some of the best white tennis players. And he won his first national tennis championship!

When he finished high school, Arthur went to the University of California at Los Angeles (UCLA). He began playing in all the big tennis tournaments.

In 1966, he won the National Collegiate Athletic Association (NCAA) singles and doubles championships. He also earned a college degree.

Arthur became a lieutenant in the Army.
He taught computer classes at West Point.
And he played tennis. In 1968, he was the
first African-American to win the U.S.
Open men's singles championship.

In 1970, Arthur won the Australian Open tournament. And in 1975, he won one of the most important tournaments of all—the Wimbledon singles championship in England.

By this time, segregation had ended in the United States. But South Africa was still a segregated country. The South African Open tennis tournament was for white players only.

In 1973, Arthur got the government of South Africa to let him play in the tournament. He hoped this would help end segregation there.

Arthur had taken one of the first steps toward speaking out against segregation in South Africa.

In 1979, when Arthur was only 36 years old, he had a heart attack. He had to have an operation on his heart. In 1980, Arthur retired from playing professional tennis.

But Arthur still coached the U.S. Davis
Cup tennis team, which plays teams from
all over the world. He helped raise money
for the American Heart Association and
the United Negro College Fund.

Arthur helped young people in cities get
involved in sports and do well in school.
He worked with groups to stop segregation
in South Africa.

Arthur got married in 1977. In 1986,
he and his wife Jeanne had a daughter.
They named her Camera.

Arthur wrote about sports for magazines and
newspapers. He talked about tennis matches
on TV. He wrote a series of books called
A Hard Road to Glory, about blacks in sports.

In 1983, Arthur had another operation on his heart. At that time, doctors were just finding out about AIDS. This disease is caused by a virus called H.I.V.

No one knew it then, but when Arthur had surgery, he probably received an H.I.V.-infected blood transfusion. In 1988, his doctors found out he had the AIDS virus. In 1992, he told the world about his illness.

AIDS takes away the body's ability to fight illness. Arthur had to take medicines to help fight off infections.

But he still worked to help African-
American teenagers compete in sports
and finish high school. And he started an
organization to help find a cure for AIDS.

In January 1993, Arthur caught pneumonia.
His family, friends, and fans all over the
world were shocked and saddened when
he died of AIDS on February 6.

Arthur's tennis championships earned him
a place in sports history. And his courage
and caring will always inspire people to do
their best to make our world a better place.